DEVIL'S MOST WANTED:
Resurrection of the FireSign

DEVIL'S MOST WANTED:
Resurrection of the FireSign

by

Candie Ferald

Devil's Most Wanted: Resurrection of the FireSign by Candie Ferald

Copyright 2022

All rights reserved. No part of this book may be used or reproduced by any means, graphic, electronic, or mechanical, including photocopying, recording, taping or by any information storage retrieval system without the written permission of the author except in the case of brief quotations embodied in critical articles and reviews.

Books authored by Candie Ferald can be ordered through PlanetCandie.com, Amazon, and other booksellers.

Cover by Randall Hamilton.

Printed in the United States of America.

Although spiritual in nature, this book contains mature subject matter that may not be suitable for children. Parental discretion is advised.

Dedicated

to

Those Who Feel Unloved.

Inspired

by

Those Who Spread Love.

**In Loving Memory of
my mother Deborah**
and
my father William

Everything is Copacetic.

Contents:

Chapter 1: The Climb..1

Chapter 2: Peace of My Pieces...33

Intermission..61

Chapter 3: FIGHT!..69

Chapter 4: When the Dust Settles...99

Alphabetical Index of Poems...129

CHAPTER 1 :

THE CLIMB

1 - My Chocolate Palm

God gave me something
  and I will hold on to it.
I will hold on to it
  like my precious life itself.
I will hold on to it
  until my very last breath.
I will hold on to it
  in spite of myself-
    even if the palm that holds it
  is all I have left.

God gave me something that
  the devil's been trying to pry away
  but I will hold on to it
  until my very last day.

I will hold on to it tightly,
  yet gently in my hands.
It won't be loosened by any storm
  nor stolen by any man.

God gave me a gift,
  meant for me and me only.
He has a plan for this child
  and I've long ago owned it.

Only He Himself knows
  how long my duty will last.
Only He Himself knows
  the specifics of my path.
My gift has outlasted my fear.

It surpasses my understanding.
I thank God everyday
  that it's been so demanding.

God gave me something
  and I will hold on to it
  despite what mayhem that comes-
  hurricanes, tornadoes, aliens, and floods,
  zombies, vampires, a pack of werewolves,
  super villains, superheroes, goblins, and trolls.
I will crush every obstacle
  on this long and unknown road...

Until Prince returns among purple rains.
Until Ali is in the ring floating again.
Until Michelle Obama loses her grace.
Until I once again, see my brother's face.

The devil will keep pressing me
  because I refuse to retract.
He will fail utterly and completely
  to deprive me of my grasp.

This gift that God gave me
  will be cocooned in the care
  of my chocolate brown hands.
It will be there in the end
  when the Earth no longer stands.

If the world is blown to pieces,
  I still won't relinquish my grip.
If nothing but ashes surround me,
  then check my fingertips.

Though an apocalypse may rob me
  of my skin, veins, and capillaries,
  you can find it among my remains.
The outcome will not vary.

My gift will last pass forever,
  overcome eternity's edge.
It will survive each and every one
  of the devil's bruising attacks.

God gave me something
  and I will hold on to it
  until from this human vessel,
  my soul has left.
I will do that in this lifetime-
  that, if nothing else.

My blessed gift will exist
  where it's lived for so long-
  nourished with faith, hope, and love
  in my grateful, chocolate palm.

2 - Killah at the Door

Let's say his name was Killah...
　...and maybe his friend was Sam.
This story involves crack rock
　and a knife in Killah's hand.

This took place one Sunday morning.
Saturday night hadn't gone as planned.
They spent that whole day partying,
　an old buddy and my Dad.
They partied a little too hard
　and ran out all their dough.
So they called up to Killah
　and asked him for a front.

He came through rather promptly.
He loaned them all that they asked.
He was to drop by in the morning
　and every dollar, he wanted back.
Things did not go that way
　the first time Killah returned.
My Dad had nothing to give him
　and he mustered no concern.
Killah left empty handed-
　infuriated he'd been burned.

He reappeared soon enough
　with his muscle Sam in tow.
Killah cut off the hallway.
Sam blocked the door.
We lived in a small trailer
　so there was nowhere left to go.

It wasn't like Dad could move.
He was couch bound and disabled.
He had just had an operation
  leaving little chance of escaping.

Killah was donning a knife
  that he was swinging all about.
He was yelling at the top of his lungs
  yet we completely tuned him out.
Maybe we were still high
  to act like we didn't care.
Our unspoken strategy-
  to pretend that they weren't there.

Killah just kept on shouting
  and we just kept watching TV.
He crept closer with that knife
  with no rise from Dad or me.
He was soon standing over my father
  fuming furiously about his cheddar.
Then suddenly there was a bang
  like a thundering firecracker.

Killah had slapped my father
  violently and in his face.
Dad's look of humiliation
  can never be erased.

We both took a deep breath.
I guess we thought Killah was through
  so we went back to ignoring him
  thinking he'd done all he was going to do.
Then Killah struck my Dad again
  even harder than he had before.

This time I saw the whole blow
  and the anger grabbed ahold.

Before I knew what was happening,
  my mouth began to shout.
It surprised even me
  that words were coming out.

I told Killah to do what he came for
  'cause there was not a dollar in the house.
I asked was he willing to kill for
  the money he thought he'd lost.
I told him to try later
  if his cash he wanted to collect.
He gave me a time for his third return
  in order to settle the debt.

I called up my brother,
  my father's oldest son.
I told him what went down
  and quickly he must come.
I told him to take my father
  to anywhere but here.
Then I called my daddy's buddy
  and made the choices very clear-
  that I needed him to bring money
  or somebody just might die.
He did what I asked before leaving.
I then waited for Killah to arrive.
I gave Killah the cash with no problem-
  no more threats, no Sam, no knife.

I might have thought on it sooner
  had I not been getting so high-

   how tragically close we came
    to losing our precious lives.

I saw Killah once after that
  across a crowded space.
He was leaving with his family
  and was oblivious to my gaze.
I wondered would he have killed us
  or had he killed before
  and what was the worst he had done.
I wondered that and more.

The saddest thing about this story
  of Killah swinging that knife.
It still wasn't enough at that time
  to stop me from getting high.

3 - Devil's Most Wanted

I used to question pretty often
  why I was made such a target,
  yet left suspiciously alone
  when I was living life in the margins.

While I was out here in this world
  drugging, corrupt, wild, and living it up.
While I was dwelling in the dark,
  there was no attempt to interrupt.

I know why it is that I'm hated,
  his deep desire that I'm utterly destroyed.
Despite the devil's efforts to conquer me,
  I wasn't designed to crumble and fold.

My bright light, he's tried to diminish.
My soul, he's viciously attacked.
I just call on God even harder
  and I trust Him to keep me on track.

Who the enemy uses can't surprise me
  so heartbreaks are less devastating.
For the prize he's waged war to obtain,
  Satan will stay wanting and waiting.

His trickery is nothing new to me.
Though by the second, he switches methods.
My spirit is supremely conditioned
  and my faith is thoroughly tested.

I must be on the devil's most wanted list.

I've obviously been there for some time.
All it took was obeying Jesus
　for the devil to straight lose his mind.

He will not shake my inheritance loose from me,
　no matter how many times I'm his target.
My loyalty is not for sale
　and my fear is off the market.

Not trying to give the devil no credit,
　he can only do what God allows.
It just seems he's at his most vicious
　when we are turning our lives around.

When we are closest to a breakthrough
　and just a leap of faith it takes,
the lying devil will try to convince you
　that believing in God is a mistake.

Seems there's a devil's most wanted list
　that I've been on for quite a spell.
If all it requires is trusting God,
　then that list suits me well.

If acting on God's Word gets me listed,
　then there's no place I'd rather be.
I will happily fight until my last breath,
　grateful for what He's done for me.

The devil has issued an all points bulletin,
　sounded a full scale, massive alarm.
He's trying to contain the armed and dangerous,
　those fueled by the All Powerful God.

He can only offer earthly rewards
  while deploying his most cunning troops
but I'm under God's protection
and guided by His truth.

If you're not on the devil's most wanted list,
  then which list are you on?
Are you inscribed among God's people
  deemed safe to leave alone?

I pray you're spreading God's love
  and not just out here for yourself.
I pray you don't fall for complacency
  and that your faith, you challenge and test.

It's not our place to judge those
  who always seem against the wall.
Inner peace doesn't happen by magic.
Sometimes it requires a brawl.

When the devil sees you as a threat,
  his pursuing you will increase.
Just keep your mind on God.
Stay wrapped in His precious peace.

The devil is by no means playing.
He's out here trying to steal some souls.
I hope to see you on the battlefield
  regardless of the earthly toll.

Being on the devil's most wanted list
  is not the position I aim or seek.
It's simply part of the journey
  when you walk by faith and won't retreat.

4 - Crack In My Foundation

Crack in my foundation,
  separated from my base.
Went to my mother's funeral
  with scratches on my face.
My eye took 7 punches.
I nearly caught a charge.
When I needed it the most,
  I got that instead of love.

I never knew how much I was hated
  'til I saw the rage in those eyes.
The fury behind those punches
  caught me completely by surprise.
I was warned something was brewing
  but that I wouldn't have thought.
I was fresh and deep into my misery
  days after losing my mom.

Crack in my foundation,
  separated from my base.
Though surrounded by my loved ones,
  I felt entirely out of place.
I had to be someone different
  to survive this attack on my heart.
Seemed I was deemed a villain
  because of the thickness of my walls.

Debates during her last days
  on how alive she was-
  though everyone clung to hope,
  I already knew that she was gone.

Drama over funeral plans-
  the best way to send her off.
Seemed my intentions were clearly doubted,
  that they came from a daughter's love.

Crack in my foundation,
  separated from my base.
As Mama's voice grew silent,
  whispers of bullshit filled the space.
While mom lay there dying,
  was told someone broke into her home-
  that some dollars came up missing
  and her new car was on the road.

Got a call while she was in the hospital
  asking if Mom had passed-
    heard someone was already in the streets
    looking for sympathy crack and cash.

Brought it up to the proper people,
  but the issue went ignored.
Only a question or two was required
  for the truth to be explored.

Crack in my foundation,
  separated from my base.
It couldn't have been planned better-
  this piling on of the pain.
I became vulnerable to the deception
  that nowhere my heart was safe
  and I became angry with the world
  but was unable to run away.

If ever I was to fold and crumble

and cease being me anymore.
If ever I was to submit to the darkness
  I had plotted to escape before.
If ever I had grown weary
  from all that I had survived.
If ever I were to even question
  was there importance to my life...

If ever existed a moment that
  my soul would cave under attack...
It would have been this moment
  when my foundation was mortally cracked.

The most unrelenting part of this feeling
  was to whom would I confide it all.
In soul trying times like this,
  I would have called my mom.

Disclaimer:
In an attempt to describe my state of mind,
  a detail was accidentally missed.
I was the one out of rage,
  who threw the very first lick.
This is where the story ends.
I gladly claim the blame.
The most important thing to know
  is that love had the final say.

5 - The Climb

I have a long road ahead of me
  but first, I must make this climb.
I've fallen into the darkness
  and sadly, it's not my first time.
The reasons are very different
  yet the darkness is the same.
Though the details somewhat vary,
  a definite pattern remains.

I took my eyes off the prize
  and I fell to the ground.
I couldn't get back up.
My pain had me bound.
The ground under me opened
  and swallowed me up whole.
I fell into the darkness,
  me and my traumatized soul.

Before I knew it,
  I was in the dark deep.
I hit the bottom.
It came up real quick.
I laid still for some moments,
  stupefied I was there.
I admit to periods of self pity
  and spells of despair.

Then something reminded me...
  I couldn't pinpoint what
  but whatever it was,
    it came roaring from my gut.

It demanded I look back
 to where it was I came from,
 that I recall all I survived
 and what I had been made of.

It reminded me of who
 my mother had been.
She was a helluva fighter.
How could I not win?
It reminded me of who
 my father had been
 and that thing that he told me.
How could I not win?

It reminded me that being a fighter
 was all up in my blood.
That I wouldn't make the climb alone,
 not as long as there lives God.

I'm in the darkness.
It ain't my first time.
I've escaped before so
 I know how to climb.

I know how to stumble.
I know how to crawl.
I know how to dig
 my fingers in the wall.
I know how to clean
 and nurse my own wounds.
I know how to cry
 when that I must do.

I know how to pause,

  to take a deep breath.
I know how to push
  when I have nothing left.
I know how to pray,
  to seek help from my Friend.
I know how to recharge
  from my Source that's within.
I know how to start over
  should I take a fall.
I know all these things
  because I've risen before.

I ain't bragging,
  just letting the enemy know.
This shit ain't over
  until God say so.

The next thing I must learn
  is how to not fall back in.
To make the lessons stick
  and not repeat this again.

To fix my foundation,
  I must identify the cracks.
I choose to move forward,
  not regress or backtrack.

But first things first and
  one thing at a time.
Inch by inch,
  I'll make this climb.

It won't be God's first miracle,
  not by my humble recollection.

I deem this chapter of my life
the FireSign's Resurrection.

6 - Sorry Set Me Free

Who wants to argue with their dead mother?
No one I know, certainly not me.
So when I felt the conflict mounting,
　I woke myself from my sleep.

At least two nights she came
　to say something in my dreams.
I didn't think I could handle
　what she had to say to me.

I just knew it would be hurtful-
　as many of our words had been.
I just knew she was about to stoke it-
　the grief already raging within.

For the six months she'd been gone,
　I tossed and turned at night.
We hadn't left things well
　and that stayed on my mind.

We often went back and forth,
　stubborn mother and stubborn daughter
　but it didn't take from the extent
　of how deeply I truly loved her.

The guilt of not feeling guilty
　for doing the best I knew how...
Who was right or wrong?
That didn't matter now.

I only wished I could tell her

that I never meant her any harm.
My vicious walls were for protection
  and weren't intended to reject her love.

I spent a lifetime feeling angry
  that I was never her first choice.
I could never quite get over losing her-
  her not loving me more than the drugs.

I only wanted a mother
  like the other little girls had-
  one who was always there for me,
  one to console me when I was sad.

One who'd tell me I was pretty
  when the world just saw my weight.
One who'd teach me about love
  before I learned the hard way.

One who the most important things
  in her life, her kids would be.
A mother who completely loved me
  and loved me just for me.

The last week she was alive,
  we had no contact at all.
She was angry with me then
  and I didn't want to stress her out.

So when she returned to me in my dreams,
  I just knew her words would wreak havoc.
I was already neck deep in darkness,
  more misery I just couldn't manage.

The first two nights I had the dream,
  I forced myself to wake up.
On the third night, she quickly stopped me
  and told me not to interrupt.

I was sitting at the front room table
  in my Grammy's house where I was raised.
My mother was standing in front of me
  holding a t-shirt to my face.

The t-shirt was a small one
  from when I was a little girl.
When I focused on the t-shirt,
  the room began to swirl.

Scenes from my childhood
  appeared through time and space.
The specifics of this t-shirt,
  I still haven't been able to place.

I had many shirts like that.
Which moment did this one depict?
Then everything was changed
  by two words from my Mama's lips.

The room stopped its spinning
  as she began to speak.
The two words she said
  were "I'm sorry"
  and her "I'm sorry" set me free.

With the two words, the dream was over
  and I continued to sleep.
For the first time since her death,

I was able to do so in peace.

I am in awe of God's power
  and the mercy of my dream.
Even from the other side,
  Mom gave me what I needed.

The circle remains unbroken.
The bond remains intact.
Though her physical form is gone,
  her presence I never lack.

7 - Land Creature

Don't want to forget how to
  hold my breath underwater...
  though my lungs yearn
  for the free and fresh air
  above the surface.
One day maybe,
  I'll even make it back to shore.

Then I can lay out on the beach
  and feel the warmth of the sunlight
  on my chocolate skin.
And maybe even take in
  the beauty of a night sky
  filled with sparkling stars
  and a moon known only in my dreams.

But right now,
  I'm still getting used to the idea
  of just keeping my head above water,
  of not being drowned by the turbulent waves
  that had me trapped underneath for so long.

I inadvertently impede my own progress.
I am so fearful that I will forget
  how to hold my breath underwater that
  I fail to give myself a proper chance
  to master the waves,
  to fully understand
  what's required to navigate them.

Too many long stories describe

how this land creature
ended up surrounded by sea waters.
So many,
  that I lose focus on the task at hand
  and I instead, get stuck on
  why my ship sank in the first place.

The task is
  to learn how to breathe
  free and fresh air again.
To make inhaling and exhaling
  that glorious air
  as much of a natural condition
  as learning how to survive
  the treacherous waters.

I must learn to stop worrying about
  life underneath the waves
  if I'm ever to flourish on land.
I'm torn between not going back under
  and making my way
  to a new life in the sand.

My lungs and all fellow body parts
  must relearn old things.
In order to survive,
  I had to suppress them
  from doing what they innately do.
I must combine old knowledge with new
  to regain my walking legs.

I find hope in the fact that
  I remember what I'm made for.
There were times when my battles

  challenged that hope
  but those challenges only fueled
  my determination to persevere.
There is a lot of life
  left for me
  to live out on the shore.
First, I must master these waves.

8 - Will to Change

I need to make a decision Lord-
  a decision that is against my will.
I need to make a decision Lord-
  a decision that is within Your will.
For a long time, I prayed Sweet Lord
  that You would make me whole,
  that You would fix the broken pieces
  and work me into Your mold.

I wish to be the me You envisioned
  at the beginning of eternity...
  so I could one day look in my mirror
  and see what it is You see.
You've provided for me and protected me.
You've guided me and deflected for me.
You stuck with me when I pushed You away.
You died for me on the cross that day.

I need to make a decision Lord-
  a decision that is against my will.
I need to make a decision Lord-
  a decision that is within Your will.

As much as I've prayed
  and asked You before,
  if I want to evolve
  I must do more-
  more than just my usual stuff.
I have to decide I've had enough
  and venture pass my comfort zone
  so into my full potential,

I may one day grow.

Help me to make that decision Lord,
  a new one this time around.
If only to prove
  solely to myself
  that I am no longer bound...
  not bound by the mistakes
  that wish to define me,
  nor by the walls
  that would like to confine me.

I need to make a decision
  that even the former me
  won't recognize.
Align me with Your will
  so that peace of mind is no surprise.

Guide me forward in progress
  even when I must stand still.
Remind me as often as needed...
  the reasons why I'm here.

And please remind me when I falter
  in trying to break old patterns...
  change is difficult to process.
It requires will to forge new habits.

I ask You for the will to change
  because You won't force it on me.
It is I who must do the choosing.
Only I am able to own it.

9 - The Company We Keep

No one says these particular words
  but they are present in their actions.
There is something dwelling inside
  demanding satisfaction.

"Hurt with me," it whispers.
"Experience some of my pain.
I'm angry at this world
  and I am trying to pull you in."

There's an entity raging inside of me.
It's poisoned many of my words.
I'm struggling to control this beast
  with which I haven't come to terms.

Some thing has been left to fester.
A wound has been left to spoil.
I've been unable to manage it.
On everything it takes a toll.

"I will take you with me," it gloats.
"You don't have to volunteer.
My path is paved in bitterness
  and I'm well equipped to steer.

"This journey will not be pleasant.
Only one solace have I found.
I can't lift myself up so
  I must pull others down."

My anger has the floor.

It is clearly the key speaker.
It's the landlord of this house.
It is the special feature.

It's drowning out my better voices,
  ensuring they'll go unheard.
It has created a sinister energy
  that has taken over my world.

This isn't who I've always been.
It's not who I want to be.
The protection created by this anger
  was a wall of safety for me.

It provided harbor from unwanted feelings
  that had taken refuge inside.
When I accepted anger's protection,
  I was unaware of its awful price.

The anger did its job.
It provided momentary relief.
Now it has taken me prisoner.
I'm not sure how to gain my release.

It will take time to reclaim my freedom
  because self change is hard to take on-
  to usher in a new way of being
  when I've survived this way for so long.

Only I can take this journey.
For each, the path is unique.
Just don't get caught in the crossfire or
  become the company that misery seeks.

Pray for me in my darkness
 until I make my escape.
Even if you must do it from a distance,
 try to love me somehow anyway.

CHAPTER 2:

♥

PEACE OF MY PIECES

1 - Toxic Ties (Never Too Late)

Some study my essence
  to try to outshine it.
They want what I have
  yet still can't define it.

They hope that my spirit
  will be eventually tamed.
They think that my resolve
  is somehow a game.

They begrudge my endurance
  not knowing its length.
They poke at my faith
  not knowing its strength.

Some huddle in the shadows
  yet live boldly in my space.
They whisper in their circles
  yet love me loudly to my face.

They've been seeking the answer
  to what makes me weak.
They drool at the chance
  to watch me get beat.

That if dealt enough blows,
  I will lose all my fight-
  that their negative predictions
  are at last proven right.

They want to be there

when I crumble and fall-
just to have a front row seat
to run tell it all.

They made a secret of their competition
  while I was cheering for their win.
They talked behind my back
  then acted like my friend.

I should've been more careful
  whom I called my friend
  but I ignored all the signs
  and got sucked right on in.

I blame it on my youth
  that I bypassed my own gut-
  that my naive instincts
  weren't developed enough.

I should've been more careful
  with whom I shared my dreams.
Some people's well wishes
  aren't as pure as they seem.

I shouldn't have chosen people
  whose insecurities had them bound-
  who only feel lifted up
  when putting others down.

It's never too late
  to cut those toxic ties.
I underestimated the influence
  of the negativity in my life.

Cut those toxic ties.
They've played enough on your mind.
Cut those toxic ties.
They've wasted too much of your time.

It's never too late
  to let that nasty energy go.
Now handle your business
  because at least now you know.

2 - A Required Role

Greetings my old friend, Grief.
I am no longer afraid of you.
Please step right on in
  and do what you came to do.

A situation requires your visit
  so let's partake in a chat.
I have something going on
  and you're well aware of that.
I invite you to a sit down
  because we must commune.
You are no stranger here
  so make yourself at home.

I'm not just inviting you in my space,
  I welcome you into my soul.
I need some of your dark magic
  to help me get back to whole.

I used to run away from you
  because I couldn't handle your vibe.
I'd do anything to avoid you.
In terrible places did I hide.

I thought you were the reason
  that I found myself in pain.
I was completely broken-hearted
  and to you, I assigned the blame.

I labeled you my enemy
  because I didn't know your role,

but you came that I might heal,
so I can manage this terrible load.

It took many times to get here-
to understand your part.
I now grant you permission
to roam through my ailing heart.

I formerly fled to darkness
and masked myself with anger.
I caved to self destruction
and created much more danger.

You're not trying to make me suffer.
The hurt was already there.
You've come to impart your process,
to lessen the anguish I bare.

You're not here to add to my pain
but you've come for its release.
You aren't supposed to stay here.
This is not your permanent place.

The sorrow that humans feel
is not meant to stick around.
You've come to ease it out
so I can stand my ground.

We have a friendship like no other
because we are both unique.
Your presence is required for closure.
Your counsel do I seek.

Your visits became more bearable

only because I invited my Friend.
He will help guide our interactions
  and ensure their proper end.

He will be right beside me
  for the duration of your stay.
He will help me consort with you
  in spiritually healthy ways.

Once our time is over,
  He will help me let you go.
So do what you came for, Grief.
Play your required role.

3 - Stopped By The Light

Strange things have time to happen
  in the seconds it takes
  for a stoplight to change.
It's usually a simple matter of
  stop, slow down or go.
It is a rather unique place
  to finally gain assurance of
    your mother's unconditional love.

Can't remember how this particular argument began.
Can't recall the particular cause.
I know at some point I confronted her
  for denying me a mother's love.

I'm sure I said many things
  though the details I can't recall.
I just know my accusation angered her.
I wasn't ready for her response at all.

Why would I say such a thing?
She immediately demanded to know.
I reminded her that I was molested
  many long years before.

I reminded her she didn't protect me.
That for me, she wasn't there.
What made it all the worse
  is she never seemed to care.

My mother wasn't having it.

She quickly put me in my place.
My words elicited her fury
  and into me, she laid.

She told me I had no idea of
  what I was talking about.
She said she hunted that babysitter,
  turning Richmond inside and out.

She said she searched everywhere
  and asked anyone she thought would know.
And when she got a lead,
  she went banging on someone's door.

She said she had planned to hurt her
  though uncertain as to how,
  that "that bitch" was quite fortunate
  that she could not be found.

She said she wanted to kill her,
  maybe choke her to death
  and that I didn't know how hard she tried
  but she surely did her best.

Even when she stopped yelling,
  her anger lingered on.
I couldn't fathom until then
  the depth of my mother's love.

What our parents do on our behalf,
  we often have no clue.
Sometimes the hardest thing for them
  is to burden us with their truth.

4 - While I Cry

I will choose a man who can hold me,
  hold me while I cry.
Until every little teardrop
  has fallen from my eyes.
Until every bead has cascaded
  and my sockets are bone dry.
I'll choose a man who can hold me
  and hold me while I cry.

He must be able to anchor me
  as sorrow makes its escape.
I need him not to judge me
  on the eternity that this may take.
His grasp must be made of patience
  and his grip, nurturing strength.
His heart must be a willing witness
  of my perseverance and its length.

This man must already realize
  that this flood doesn't mean I'm weak.
He'll recognize how long I've been strong
  and that I well deserve relief.
I need him to politely ignore
  his drenched and snot-ridden sleeves.
I need his only concern to be
  that he's in the moment with me.

And this man's arms can make it better
  as my tears consume his shoulders.
Let him squeeze me in reassurance
  that he will be here when it's over.

I need this man to hold me
  while I dispel my pains.
His care will help ease them out
  and send them on their way.

As the tears claim their form,
  I need him to not be scared.
Let his love serve as armor
  while my soul is naked and bare.
He'll even completely understand
  if all that crying leads to laughter.
Considering the parade of tears,
  I've earned the peace that comes after.

And certainly he won't be the reason
  that my weary pipes have burst.
The honor of sharing my anguish
  comes after he's earned my trust.
These are some requirements
  where men and my heart collide.
If he can't withstand my darkness,
  he is not worthy of my light.

5 - Peace of My Pieces

I am a partly finished masterpiece,
  a puzzle
  that was knocked down
  to the floor.
All of my pieces
  scattered everywhere.
My reality did implode.

Pieces landed all over the place.
I was immobilized by the shock.
When at last I was ready to reassemble myself,
  I began to gather them up.

There were a myriad of different pieces
  that comprised my composition.
I hoped I could again learn to trust myself
  to arrange them in their rightful position.

Some pieces were strong and beautiful,
  others weak and vulnerable to the touch.
Which pieces were essential to my being?
Had I developed the wisdom to judge?

Some pieces were tethered and worn
  and had suffered extensive damage.
The emotional work needed for repair,
  I had to summon the strength to manage.

Some pieces seemed quite new to me,
  parts of myself I had not yet noticed.
I learned I owed it to all of myself

to give them some love and focus.

Upon further examination,
  some pieces were quite a surprise
  and answered long opened questions
  when seen through my new set of eyes.

Some pieces no longer fit
  the person I had chosen to be.
I had to learn to let them go
  to become my preferred version of me.

The enormity of the task often overwhelmed me.
Faith in myself would sometimes flee.
If I'd formerly made such a mess of things,
  how dare I dream to be free?

I met patience through this process.
It required that I face all of my truths-
  to craft each and every hardship survived
  into a woman exquisitely new.

What would become of the empty spaces
  that had been formerly made of pain?
If so much of me is missing,
  how would I ever be whole again?

Do I keep old pieces just 'cause they'd been there
  through more than I care to recall?
Do I reject new ones in suspicion,
  unclear how they scaled my walls?

And what if I don't get this right?
A plethora of questions filled my mind.

Remembering God drew up my design
  is what makes my fears subside.

As this good work in me continued,
  a revelation came to my soul...
  that this chance to change was a blessing
  that God surely wants me to enjoy.

Turns out the masterpiece that is forming
  is more spectacular than the one in my mind.
It's funny how things had to fall apart
  before inner peace, my pieces could find.

6 - The Prime Directive

I reconnected with something in myself
  during my travels back...

Travels back of introspection
  to examine pieces of myself
  as they previously were.
To see my old self
  with my new eyes.
Trying to dissect
  my own inner mechanisms
  for some fine tuning and repair.

I rediscovered and reconnected with something
  that was buried so deep inside
  it had become a natural part of me.
So deep I had almost forgotten
  that it wasn't always there.
It had fastened itself to my core,
  this mindset and it refused to move
  no matter how hard life circumstances
  tried to shake it loose.

It was the goal to always be happy,
  to seek and incorporate things in my life
  that would encourage and elicit my God given joy.
True happiness...
  not the superficial,
  artificial satisfaction with things
  that could be here today and gone tomorrow.
Not the momentary response when life goes my way
  but the deep seated euphoria and harmony of inner peace

regardless of the world outside.

Happiness that defies the sadness and anger of others.
Happiness that serves as a spectacular reflection
  of the unconditional and boundless love of God.
I sought happiness in places
  where others failed to look.
At one time, I sought it even when
  what made me happy
  wasn't always healthy.

The goal of happiness was given to me by my mother.
I can't remember my exact question
  or what I had asked or what I said
  but I do clearly remember her response...
  that whatever I did,
  whatever I chose,
  all she wanted for me
  out of this life
  was "to be happy".

She said it with no hesitation and in such a way
  that it didn't seem like a request.
She didn't use "be" as a passive or state of being verb.
She used "be" as an action verb
  easily implying that
  this directive would require effort.
And she did not use "happy" as just a simple adjective.
In fact, she offered no definition of "happy" at all.
She left the defining up to me...
  just that I be it.
"Happy"- the prime directive
  from this mother to her daughter.
She planted that seed deeply

and it immediately took root.

The quest for happiness seems such an obvious thing
  but the evidence of anger, depression,
  and sadness in this world suggests
  that a journey of true happiness
  has become overrated and undervalued to many.
Looking around,
  I began to understand the meaning of my quest,
  that happiness doesn't always just come around.
That for many and most it must be found,
  gathered and nourished
  and made to fit
  one's own individual self.

To realize happiness requires work.
It wouldn't easily fall into my lap.
I would learn that
  some things that effortlessly gratify
  are actually just traps.
I began to understand
  that though happiness is part of my being,
  we would sometimes become estranged
  and I would need to learn to recognize it.
So that when it wandered away,
  I could gather it close again.

Many don't think so intently on the concept of happiness.
Many have had it defined for them by someone else
  and have yet to explore each aspect
  of that definition for themselves.
They have yet to challenge it,
  let alone,
  create and live their own version of it.

I'm so thankful for this prime directive
  that my Mom sealed in place.
The joy that came from that seed
  still blossoms to this day.
It remains firmly rooted
  and intertwined with my core.
Mom's profound and beautiful gift,
   her prime directive, has shaped my soul.

7 - It Was The Laughter

It was the laughter that did it.
It was the laughter that changed my course.
It was that laughter that called out to me-
   that I should never lose my voice.

Especially before I discover its tone
   or hear what it has to say.
It was the laughter that warned me
   to take great care in how I changed.

This country girl moved to the city.
It was my freshman year in college.
I was eager to experience things
   beyond classroom knowledge.

It was an intro to all kinds of characters.
One shined brightly among them all,
   the first name many learned,
   one of the most popular kids in the dorm.

He bubbled over with laughter.
He spread it everywhere he went.
He was never found without it,
   an undeniable part of him.

Gut busting, side splitting laughter,
   the pant peeing, catch your breath sort-
   the kind to leave you in tears,
   laughing so hard it hurts.

That was also my kind of laughter,

the kind I'd always known.
  I never thought it was one of those things
  that could be here one day, then gone.

We were carefree and naive,
  the world full of bright tomorrows.
We were eager to learn to navigate it,
  to manifest and wield our power.

Somehow in his growing,
  that young boy who was so full of life,
  lost more and more of his laughter
  as each of the four years passed by.

Whatever caused him to lose his-
  I didn't want to happen to me.
I hadn't even begun to define myself
  but knew laughter was a central piece.

I didn't want to change too much
  before finding out who I was.
I had to know that what I stood to gain
  was worth what I was giving up.

I began observing my classmates,
  taking note of how they changed and grew.
The ones who had lost their laughter
  were more likely to be donning suits.

They were preparing for a new world
  that required them to fit in some box-
  that told them how they needed to be
  while leaving out what it might cost.

Now they barely even chuckled
  while I still needed to laugh real hard.
The thought of losing that part of myself
  set off all kinds of alarms.

So I decided to follow the laughter,
  to make its abundance a mark of success.
I swore to not take the path
  that would rob me of my happiness.

Many will try to shape you
  into who they think you should be.
You decide what remains intact
  and laughter was a choice for me.

I wonder where that boy is now-
  and if he has regained his laughter.
And if by chance it remains estranged,
  was it worth what he was after?

8 - Black Versus Black

I guess she must have googled me
  because she never called.
Maybe she determined
  I wasn't the right kind after all.

No, not the right kind of person
  but not the right kind of black.
It left me to wonder...
  what the hell kind of black is that?

Of all the options and alternatives
  of the type of person I choose to be,
  I thought the melanin in my skin
  had decided black for me.

Is there some kind of black
  from which my melanin has me excluded?
Who laid out the qualifications
  and exactly which blacks are included?

What are the criteria
  to determine which black is correct?
And who will choose the expert
  to administer that kind of test?

There are many kinds of black.
I wouldn't dare try and name them all.
Endless ways we manifest the culture
  of the chocolate rainbow we belong.

Infinite tones and tastes

comprise our multi-coated race.
From unspeakable horrors,
  our bond is forever made.
We carry both
  the strength and trauma
  of descendants of brutalized slaves.

We have no room for colorism
  when there are some who'd kill us all.
They despise every black person
  despite where on the spectrum they fall.

Being shockingly referred to as upper
  though my means say otherwise.
Because of my proper talk,
  been told I thought I was white.

Been treated as an outcast
  because I didn't act black enough.
Been treated as if I'm guilty
  for not reaching a higher rung.

Been given looks of disdain
  because I wear my hair in braids.
Been regarded like I'm less than
  because I haven't refined my ways.

I prefer my hair as natural.
Weave just ain't my thing.
Should I be giving a sista the stank eye
  for wearing her crown different than me?

Light skin versus dark skin.
House versus field slave.

Maybe we judge each other
  to avoid facing our legacy's pain.

What and where we come from
  is branded deeply in our hearts.
Our people helped build a free country
  but we still can't be who we are.

Some run from the pain of our history.
Some focus on victory and gain.
Some still can't reconcile it
  and slavery is too simple a name.

Some are still stuck in a cycle.
Others want to deny it was there.
Trying to prove which black is best
  is a burden we needlessly bare.

Being the right kind of black,
  according to what someone deems?
How about I just be the kind of person
  that allows me to be my best me?

Must I minimize my experiences
  to fit in some tiny box?
Haven't blacks all over the world
  been through more than enough?

Is someone the right kind of black
  should never be a question.
Anyone who needs to ask that
  is grappling with their own reflection.

9 - Automatic Entry

I must have said something crazy
  as I often tend to do
  because my Cuz laughed and looked at me
  and said girl, "Something's wrong with you!"

Yup, something sure is wrong-
  if I must be completely honest
  but I am in good company
  because something is "wrong" with all of us.

I've learned to laugh at myself,
  to poke fun at my silly quirks.
When there are more serious problems,
  I do the spiritual work.

When it seemed to be a fatal flaw,
  I empowered myself to change it.
When I didn't like where life was headed,
  I took steps to rearrange it.

No one, no soul, not one single body
  has it completely all together.
There exists not a single being
  without one naughty pleasure.

Some habits may be a little naughtier
  while some seem more benign.
Some lifestyles seem more natural
  while others wouldn't cross my mind.

What makes others feel good-

their slight, little defect
doesn't negate God's commandment
to love them as I love myself.

And no, I present no confessions.
Y'all don't need to know all I do.
But if something is wrong with me,
　then there's something wrong with you.

Somewhere inside each of us
　lies an incurable imperfection.
I wear mine as a badge of humanity
　rather than letting it dull my reflection.

As long as it's not stifling me
　or hindering another's route,
　I just enjoy that piece of myself.
It's been freeing embracing my truths.

When I've tried to deny what comes natural,
　I've been easily turned around.
Just some of the things I find natural,
　I can't discuss in any old crowd.

Self hate due to my imperfections
　of which others may disapprove
is a burden I no longer shoulder,
　something I'm unwilling to do.

So whatever you think you know of me,
　whether I shared it or you surmised-
　know that self acceptance is serious business
　and is not contingent on any vice.

My brain is sometimes flighty.
I'm not a stranger to being bossy.
My mouth runs pretty smart
  and I'm definitely prone to naughty.

So yup, something is wrong with me.
You too, are in this club.
Whatever issues you may have,
  don't let one be lack of love.

INTERMISSION:

There is a super long poem in the middle of this book.

Fat, Black, and Smart:
The Acquisition of Adjectives

For most of my childhood,
  I thought only three words
  defined all of who I was.
Just three.

I was fat, black, and smart...
  just those three things.

Only one of those things I knew to be good
  and it wasn't being fat or widespread yellow or fat ass fucker
  or whatever nasty thing a person wanted to say out their mouth.
Kids could be cruel but adults could be worse.
Many hurtful times, I looked up to one
  only to have them join in on all the fun
  spouting slick remarks they thought were cute.
Even little kids know when they are the punchline.

"Oooh, you have such a pretty face,"
  as if the rest of me, particularly my fat body,
  was forever a lost cause.
As if that not really a compliment
  gave them permission to give me the up and down
  so they could gather in all my fatness.
Right in front of my such a pretty face
  as if my eyes couldn't follow theirs,
  as if my body didn't feel like it was being inspected
  or was on display in some freak show.

I wonder if there would've been less teasing
  if people knew I was an emotional eater...
  eating to hide hurt and fear that as a child,

I didn't possess the words to express.
That hurt and fear was deep.
The teasing didn't help so I ate even more.
I later developed some promiscuous ways.
I was desperate to prove that a person
   could be fat and desirable all at the same time-
   the complete opposite
   of what had been drilled into my head and heart.
Perhaps that was the beginning
   of me learning how to use instead of how to love.

I knew that being black wasn't too hot either.
While my Mom played bingo,
   my little sister and I were chased by kids
   pointing their BB guns at us
   yelling "shoot them niggers"*
   in the bright and broad daylight
   on a main street in the next town over.
That was my first clue that being black wasn't safe,
   not even in the bright and broad daylight.

One of my favorite preteen things to do
   was to skate at the Friday night skate rink
   on the edge of my hometown.
I looked forward to it every week…
   so maybe it was being called a nigger*
   by a bunch of older kids whizzing by
   that also signaled the lack of safety in being black.
I was scared to tell my Mom what happened…
   scared of what she might do
   and scared of what would then be done to her.
I never went back to that skating rink
   and I never told her the real reason why.

Or maybe it was the talk that many black families
  have with their black babies
  of the importance
  of not giving the wrong kind of white folks
  a single reason to think that
  you were what they thought
  was the wrong kind of black.
It's hard enough for a child to be their true selves
  without having to tiptoe through the muck of racism.
Knowing that black folks were often terrorized
  for standing up for themselves
  and that we lived miles from town
  where no one would hear our screams
  added to that fear.

It was an anomaly
  when people who looked like me
  had money, lived in big pretty houses,
  were on TV, or won beauty pageants.
No, black was not the thing to be,
  not if you wanted to live without limits
  or to simply feel safe.

Being smart was supposed to be a good thing.
Too often though,
  I found myself pigeonholed
  by the strength of my own intelligence...
  something that was supposed to set me free.
Being smart was the best thing that I was
  because everything else was too far away.
Too fat to be pretty,
  too black to be successful,
  too guarded to be liked,
  too different to be accepted.

So I had to be smart
  because there were no other available options.
I was often held to impossible standards
  by adults, peers and even so called friends
  that an impressionable child
  should never be expected to reach.
I grew scared to ask questions
  because not knowing the answers
  meant that the one good thing I was,
  I wasn't even that.

Knowing everything was never the definition of smart.
Still, some couldn't wait for me to fall short.
They reveled when I didn't know everything,
   taunting me that I wasn't as smart as I was led to believe.
This was pretty devastating to someone
  who was just trying to be herself
  and before their teasing,
  thought they actually liked me.
I learned that I had to be right about everything,
  that there was no room for error.
I became my own worst enemy.
I denied myself permission to love myself
  when I faltered.
Self love had become too intertwined with being smart.

Book sense but no common sense was my Mom's favorite.
I couldn't help but to feel different
   if common sense was something everyone else had except me.
Funny, I don't ever remember taunting those
  with common sense for not having enough book sense.

Fat, black, and smart-
My journey towards self knowledge started with those three words,

words that told me what I was but not who.
For the sake of self preservation,
  I gathered the best from them and
    acquired the fine art of making those words work for me.

I learned that being smart wasn't just about
  what you knew or how to apply it.
It also meant that because I exercised my brain regularly,
  I became a fast learner,
    an invaluable trait for someone so thirsty for knowledge.
Once I learned that I could learn anything,
  doors opened that I hadn't even considered knocking on.

My fat became thick and voluptuous.
Men still fawn over my big, chocolate legs
  and the curves and fullness of my female places.

Being shunned so much, I had to learn to love my insides first
  and that inner beauty is far more important than outer.
I had to learn who I was and
  to think deeply on who I wanted to be.
I had to learn to love myself even if no one else ever would.
Some people never learn these lessons
  and I was blessed to do so early.

I've concluded that my blackness is a source of strength.
I've only brushed the surface of my profound history.
There is power in knowing that though chained,
  my ancestors still nourished and instilled hope.
My blackness is a beauty, of the celestial sort.
My naturally curly, nappy, thick hair is
  what God gave me and
  it grows out and upward
  as in a crown.

Once I flipped the script,
  I became excited and determined to acquire more adjectives.
  This time, I would be the sole authority...
  exercising my God given free will and employing His guidance.
I am grateful for the privilege of self definition and
  I look forward to the continued evolution of
  my much longer list of me.

Please note that my use of this word is not permission or approval for people not of color to also use this word. I offer no explanations because I won't and I shouldn't have to.

CHAPTER 3:

FIGHT!

1 - Tainted

Tainted is how I'd describe it,
  knowing the word is pretty harsh.
That piece of paper is Lord knows where.
It was never worthy of my walls.

Every time I think of it,
  I'm reminded of what I lost-
  of what I wish I'd known back then
  and what my ignorance cost.

My degree was supposed to mean something
  but it reflects a me that I hated.
It took just one afternoon
  for that prized degree to become tainted.

I was completing my honor's thesis.
With a few months left 'til graduation,
  the professor asked to meet with me.
It was a heart breaking conversation.

He said I was no longer being aided
  by my mentor since first semester.
The mentor hurtfully dropped me.
I had made an unwitting error.

Impressed by his colleague's speech,
  I asked for her thoughts on my work.
I didn't berate my mentor
  and didn't know I had to ask him first.

I wasn't hip to the politics

that led to my mentor's defection.
My professor then took over
  and pushed me to change directions.

I felt like a pawn between rivals,
  that somehow I was owned.
My ignorance caused this dismissal
  when I had done nothing wrong.

I had earned all A's in my major.
Now the professor was giving me a C.
He had had two semesters
  to lay that news on me.

He had had two semesters
  to tell me I was off track,
  to be a good professor,
  to inform me of what I lacked.

It was a two semester course.
Time and opportunity were there.
Imagine my curious surprise
  that he picked this moment to care.

The professor then gave me a choice,
  a startling decision to make.
I could take my C and go
  or wait to graduate.

That C would be the difference
  between Summa and Magna Cum Laude.
After four years of my hard work,
  the rug was pulled from under me.

As the professor spoke,
  it seemed he was holding back.
I hadn't learned how to stand up for myself
  and I didn't know what I needed to ask.

I surely didn't trust him enough
  to admit why my plans were made.
I wanted to be close to my mom
  who I thought certain to die of AIDS.

I was moving home for graduate school.
I was to start the following fall.
To alter my plan at this point...
  too many reasons not to make that call.

I couldn't bring myself to tell my people
  that I let this happen to me.
They never understood the reason
  I didn't cherish my degree.

Don't assume each trip through college
  is an easy ride.
I built up even more walls
  when I should've just let myself cry.

Necessity created a fierce independence.
I couldn't always tell when I needed help.
Though I was always surrounded,
  it felt like I was out there by myself.

Now that lost piece of paper is
  just a token from lifetimes ago.
That describes the extent
  of the positive sentiment it holds.

I experienced many wonders in school
  that this situation did not diminish.
Yet the way in which I was handled
  cast a shadow over my finish.

I hoped that by finally letting it out,
  I would feel somewhat better.
But nope, not a thing has changed.
That piece of paper is as tainted as ever.

2 - The Most Detrimental

I wanted to be an activist-
  that's what I should have said.
That desire never found a voice
  because I was afraid.
I wanted to be like Malcolm-
  to bring about positive change,
  but I was too scared to speak on
  what made me feel that way.

Casting blame is not my intent.
This happens in families all the time.
Quieting me wasn't meant to hurt
  but to protect our peace of mind.

The silence meant to shield
  bore a greater cost.
With the suppression of my voice,
  more than some hopes were lost.

It wasn't just about sharing dreams
  but seeking and accepting help.
With the suppressing of my developing voice,
  I struggled to express myself.

Nor did I feel free to seek advice
  with issues that had me troubled.
I didn't want to betray my family.
So silently, I suffered.

What goes on in the house stays there.
It's not even remotely that simple.

An awful burden falls on the children
  inadvertently caught in the middle.

They can't always grasp what's going on
  and lack the words to explain if they did.
If it's devastating for the adult,
  imagine how it feels to the kid.

The trauma just doesn't go away.
There's no wave of a magic wand.
Those ignored emotions become toxic
  when left to fester too long.

Trapped with me inside the walls I built,
  the rage fed upon my soul.
That and the depression it caused
  found release when I would explode.

What looked to others as just anger
  was the only way I knew how to cope.
It took decades to work through my layers,
  to finally let that rage go.

The fear of public embarrassment
  obstructs healing all the time.
You don't have to tell it all,
  but you can't fix what you deny.

The quieting was for our protection.
The consequences were accidental.
Of the things that didn't go right,
  that silence was the most detrimental.

The craziest thing about this practice

is that many families do the same thing.
Imagine how better the world would be
　if so many weren't hindered by their shame.

What is the healthy balance
　between privacy and expression?
Whichever proves best for the soul,
　I err in that direction.

I pray that my loved ones forgive me
　if they are bothered by these words.
I'll gladly deal with that result
　if at least one hurting child is heard.

I remain eternally grateful
　for the infinite ways they blessed my life.
But the enemy hid in that silence.
It is to him, I take my fight.

3 - Not That Kind of Fence

I'm sorry if someone hurt you,
  made you want to turn away from God.
I'm sorry if you thought their nastiness
  was directed from up above.

Some duck behind the Bible
  to feel superior to others.
They pick and choose their verses,
  whichever grants them comfort.

They pick and choose the words
  that compliment their vision,
  yet won't step out on faith
  to pursue God given missions.

They'd rather blame the outside
  than face the work within.
They're missing their opportunities
  to fight their fears and win.

Some only use the Bible
  to throw in another's face,
  reciting selected passages
  to assign people to their place.

With some folks all that reading
  doesn't go beyond the words.
It is invisible in their demeanor
  and absent in their verbs.

God didn't give us His Word

  to tear each other apart.
The Good News should unite and guide us,
  to strengthen our wanting hearts.

Some hide behind the Bible
  thinking that's all they need to learn.
They won't offer sympathy to others
  yet expect it when the tables turn.

He told us we should testify
  but many can't stand to hear it.
If the story follows foreign lines,
  some fear going anywhere near it.

God's Word is not that kind of fence-
  to belittle others as we peer over.
It's a wall of spiritual protection
  for when our souls are in need of cover.

God speaks in many ways,
  not just through biblical pages.
He exists in all His creations,
  yet shows us many faces.

I don't have all the answers.
It's fine that I never will.
But I know better than to use religion
  to try and beat out my brothers' sins.

I hope a person wasn't the reason
  you turned and walked away from God.
Don't let anger at someone else
  cause you to miss out on all His love.

And if you are a believer
  who misuses His words to hurt-
  don't forget the ones you're damaging,
  God has deemed our equal worth.

4 - An Acceptable Dose

My heart struggles hopelessly
  and is unable to reconcile
  how people you know are kind
  can uplift a thing so vile.
When those you know are good
  didn't just look aside
  but by their deliberate actions
  have helped that evil to rise.

What could possibly be
  in the back of their minds
  that their conflicting choice
  they justify?

Is it that...

What is a little bit of racism
  when proven what a group can take?
Surely everything is an improvement
  over forced labor, brutality and rape.
Those things are way less tolerated
  but it doesn't mean racism was lost.
It just means that it is now dispensed
  into more socially "acceptable" doses.

And isn't that certainly a step up
  compared to being slaves?
And because it's not as blatant,
  doesn't that make it more OK?
Oh...what's a little bit of racism
  after what our ancestors endured?

How dare we be so ungrateful?
How dare we strive for more?

Many former acts of horror
　that most agree were inhumane,
　were replaced by modern versions
　but their intent is quite the same.
Pointy white sheets with eye holes
　were replaced with something new.
It is by no means absolution
　showing love to a certain few.

We've had one black president
　so we've obviously come some ways.
Yet equality is a full meal
　of which we've only had a taste.
To then give someone so much power
　who discriminates based on race...
　how can you expect people of color
　to not feel dismissed or betrayed?

It poured salt on racial wounds
　that were finally starting to heal-
　as if the bonds of true community
　some never want us to feel.
A lifetime of working twice as hard
　to earn chances that some are given.
Opportunities passed right by me
　because I didn't fit the description.

Systemic racism runs rampant
　in many of our institutions.
Some prefer it just like that
　so they fight against solutions.

Should I accept racial injustice
  as just a little tick in the system
  and if it ain't as bad as slavery
  is it really worth the mention?

Does it seem more acceptable
  when by dog whistles, it's disguised?
Does it seem more acceptable
  if you can pretend that you're surprised?
Does it seem more acceptable
  if no one shed their blood?
Does it seem more acceptable
  for other neighborhoods?

What is that acceptable dose of racism-
  how much you think won't harm?
Where do you draw the line?
What causes your conscience alarm?

We hail our beautiful country
  as the greatest democracy.
Shouldn't that mean each citizen
  be equally safe and free?

How do you see your part?
How will you cast your vote?
How do you think you'll get me to swallow
  what you deem an acceptable dose?

5 - The Persistent Caller

I have a persistent caller
  trying to get me on the line.
I do my best to ignore him
  yet he insists on some of my time.

The caller is no good for me.
He's proven that for sure.
When I listen to his lies,
  the results are hard to endure.

It doesn't pay to be polite
  in the ways that I refuse.
The caller knows me well.
Any weakness he's apt to use.

I can take the phone off the ringer.
He'll find another connection.
He knows what has meaning to me
  and whom I hold with love and affection.

He's acquainted with all my deeds.
With my sorrows, he's quite familiar.
He remains always close to me,
  ever present in my mirror.

He calls on me as I am sleeping.
He interrupts me during the day.
He thinks we should be inseparable
  and proceeds to act that way.

My caller reeks nothing but havoc,

takes pride in utter destruction.
He consumes all I have and
  contributes absolutely nothing.

My caller is a parasite
  who wants entrenchment in my core.
He has but one objective-
  that I surrender my soul.

It doesn't matter if I change my number
  as I've done many times before.
He won't give up until he reaches me,
  until he completes his revolting goal.

It seems the only course of action
  is proactive interception-
  that I remain keenly aware of
  his channels and his methods.

He aims to poison my happy space
  and strangle out all my joy,
  to separate me from my strengths,
  to leave me empty and void.

He wants me to forget there exists
  healthy means to pleasure.
He insists that I submit to him
  my life's truest treasures.

His siege will not be over
  until I declare him king.
For that one and only purpose,
  he's willing to do anything.

This dilemma isn't a new one.
It's been like this for a while.
The caller quite enjoys this-
  the power he has in my life.

Many have fallen victim
  and even more battle bravely on.
He's unfortunately made himself comfortable
  in many a human home.

My persistent caller prefers to stay hidden.
In secret, are his greatest gains.
The first step in defeating him
  is to know depression is his name.

.

6 - Tap In

My sister burst into my room one day.
I was planted on the edge of my bed.
She said that I had been stuck that way
  since the water sign had passed.

It had been two long, brutal weeks-
  a sudden death of the young it was.
I was feeling nothing but brokenness
  when it was that I didn't feel numb.

Don't think it had been two years
  since I had escaped my addiction
  and I was still unsteady from
  the remnants of that affliction.

The world seemed full of sadness.
My heart was replete with doom.
After dragging myself to work each day,
  I'd come home to hide in my room.

My sister burst straight through the door
  and demanded I somehow move.
She said she didn't know what to say
  or even less, what she could do.

I could tell my sister meant business.
I could see the worry in her eyes.
I had to think of something quick
  so I could mobilize.

"Don't forget to count your blessings,"

I could hear my Grammy's voice.
I needed to regain my strength
　so I tapped into my power Source.

I thought maybe I'd feel stronger
　if at least ten blessings I could name,
　to give God thanks for what I have-
　my joy I was trying to reclaim.

As crazy as it may seem,
　I started with the little things-
　objects right in front of me
　that I could plainly see.

I thanked God for the clothes
　that were thrown about my floor.
I thanked God I had a floor
　that I could throw them on.

I thanked God I had my own place
　where I could rest my head
　because just two years before,
　I was resting it anywhere.

I thanked God for the places
　I had slept during my addiction
　and that He still had a plan for me
　and a path to complete my mission.

God had kept me safe.
It could have went the other way.
I thanked God for my survival
　and the chance of another day.

I was just trying to count to ten
  but the list of blessings kept on flowing.
If tears hadn't had me choking,
  I'd probably still be going.

I can truly testify
  counting my blessings has never failed.
That when pain seeks your weakness,
  God's faithfulness will prevail.

Jesus is the Light within when
  I'm feeling desperately loss.
He is free and I don't have to go nowhere
  to plug into my power Source.

Jesus didn't promise a lack of misery.
He never promised that life would be fair.
I learned He meant it when He said it-
  that through it all, He would always be there.

The there is right here inside of me,
  exactly where He's always been.
I simply start by counting my blessings
  anytime I need to tap in.

7 - One Enemy

There is one lone and singular enemy
  which each human shares.
He bombards us with distractions
  so we'll forget he's even there.
Not your average, everyday enemy
  but an eternal, formidable foe,
  one who has few limits and
  plots to devour us whole.

We call others our enemies
  when we fail to get along
  but this one enemy of which I speak
  is the evil behind each wrong.
Any injustice and misery we can think of,
  in him the source resides.
He is the chief mischief maker,
  the indisputable father of lies.

Yet this enemy can't defeat us
  without us defeating ourselves.
The enemy can't defeat us
  without our very own help.
The enemy has to get in our heads
  to taint what we believe.
He preys on our vulnerabilities
  so we will bend to hate and fear.

To blame others for our problems
  when they have plenty of their own.
He'll plant any little reason
  for us to hate another soul.

He wants us to look over our shoulders
  so that we can't look ahead,
  to rob us of our present joy
  and immobilize us with dread.

The enemy has been plotting
  since even before time began.
The enemy seeks to divide us.
Don't lend him a helping hand.
He wants us to withhold forgiveness,
  to believe people can never change.
He wants that when we're injured,
  we react by returning the pain.

He wants us to forget our bravery
  when we face our human fears.
He wants us to think we're alone
  in managing our burdens and tears.
He wants us to think that to be loved,
  we must be as perfect as perfect can be.
He wants us to believe God is distant
  and that the real us, He can't see.

He needs us to turn on one another
  so we will cause each other pain,
  to weaken what is good inside
  so we will lose our hope and faith.
Don't take out on fellow humans
  fury better reserved for him.
Please play your important part
  to help usher in God's win.

Know that Satan is that one enemy
  trying to pull us away from God.

Know that everything the devil offers
  is the complete opposite of love.

Knowing the ways that he gets to us
  better readies us for the fight.
The most prolific weapon we have
  is to treat fellow humans right.

God gave us the gift of one another
  so we don't have to fight alone.
Jesus paid the price.
Yet, the war rages on.

☙ - FIGHT!

Some have lost their children
  and will never hold them again.
Many were helplessly there
  and witnessed the unspeakable end.

Some have survived a terror
  by laying in their loved one's blood.
There are some whose very mistakes
  caused their beloved to be lost.

Some went to work whole one morning
  and never made it back home.
Some went to school whole one morning
  and their whereabouts are still unknown.

Some came in this world missing limbs,
  others arrived with blinded eyes.
Some never knew their mom or dad
  and some babies were just left to die.

Some have been ravaged by disease.
Some have fallen prey to addiction.
Some have been victims of violence
  and then were failed by the system.

Some were sent off to war
  and have horror etched in their minds.
They carry in their souls every day
  trauma they couldn't leave behind.

Some little kids have been brutally raped

before they even knew what it was.
Some have lived most of their life
  oppressed by their emotional scars.

Each human shoulders a burden
  under which they could crumble and fall.
The weight of what we can bare
  is very different to each and all.

Name that burden that you carry-
  the pain that corrodes your might.
Summon what's left of your reserves
  and get yourself up and fight!

A moment may be required to rest,
  some time needed to rearrange.
Know there is at least one task left
  as long as a breath remains.

Fight for the survival of goodness
  in places where evil reigns.
Fight so that today's youth
  don't have to repeat our sins.

Someone who's close to giving up
  just might find hope in you.
Fight so that the path is kinder
  for the next traveler to pursue.

Fight so that all your sufferings
  somehow seem worth the pain.
Fight so that from your mistakes,
  the devil has less ground to gain.

Fight to be an example
  of how love's power carries on.
Fight in absolute confidence
   that the victory is already God's.

Fight with the gifts God gave you-
   the mission to spread His love
   so regardless of what each endures,
   no one has to endure it alone.

Fight!
Knowing that someone somewhere
   would give anything for one more chance.
Fight!
Knowing that what you believe in
   is unquestionably worth taking a stand.

Don't you ever give up on life's wondrous things
   often buried under stress and strife.
Because your Creator does not dole out fear
   but the power and authority to fight.

9 - Do Me No Favors

To imply being faithful is a favor
  is to imply that it is not deserved.
That only flies with women
  shaky in regards to their worth.
I won't lend weight to the excuse
  that men were built to roam,
  that they can freely sow their oats
  while women are meant to stay home.

Promiscuous women are whores
  that can never make good wives.
Promiscuous men are just playboys
  and it's a natural part of life.
Who came up with this bullshit?
Who ordained these rules?
Who claims to be the ultimate authority
  on what men versus women should do?

Bowing to these double standards
  is to divide yourself in parts.
If parts of you lie all over the place,
  then where dwells your full heart?
Have you decided you're so much of a man
  you can be divided into portions?
Have you decided that I'm not worthy
  to receive your complete devotion?

And if you are a full entity
  and I'm only getting half,
  does that make me less than whole
  if you logically follow the math?

Do you see me as only a fraction
   of what your ideal woman should be?
Have you truly put forth the effort
   to explore the ins and outs of me?

Your faithfulness is not a favor.
You say forgiveness is what I owe.
But don't you owe me loyalty?
Isn't that too, a component of love?
These questions that I ask of you,
   you should probably ask yourself.
If you really believe in our love
   then why would you trade it for less?

You say that...
   if I love you,
   how could I walk away?
I say that...
   if you loved me,
   how could you so easily stray?

Chronic infidelity
   is the symptom, not the cause.
It indicates that somehow
   you never learned the meaning of love.
And if this is your version of love...
   the best way you know how,
   then maybe there is a time for us
   but that time can not be now.

Our ending does not have to be nasty
   but it most certainly has to be.
My future man will treat it as privilege
   to get to love the hell out of me.

CHAPTER 4:

WHEN THE DUST SETTLES

1 - Unapologetic Ambition

No apologies for being better
   than you think I ought to be.
No apologies for not deferring
   to your limited version of me.

No one will dissuade me
   from the dreams I choose to pursue.
I won't water down my fire
   to appear less dazzling to you.

No regrets for determination-
   that I won't give up my fight.
I won't deny my vision
   because it doesn't suit your sight.

I won't dumb down my smarts
   to put your mind at ease.
If my imagination surpasses yours,
   you won't take it out on me.

I won't relinquish my power.
Instead, I'll build on its source.
I do not need your two cents.
It has never been your choice.

It's obvious this is news to you-
   as if you've never been told.
Maybe no one has put it so plainly-
   that your judgment is nasty and old.

You may need some adjustment time

and that is not my problem.
Maybe if you put forth the effort,
   you'd benefit from your own evolving.

I do not seek your approval.
Your permission is not required.
Your hating is quite ludicrous
   and my patience is long expired.

Don't wait on me to answer you.
For what reasons do you pose
   that somehow your opinion of me
   should be my greatest goal?

Just like God gave you yours,
   I've my own brain, body, and soul.
The fact that I have to tell you this
   means you have ways to go.

Don't litter my path with negativity
   because your yard has gathered weeds.
Don't throw salt on my garden.
Mind your own thirsty seeds.

Your great attention to my ambitions
   imply a lack of confidence in your own.
I hope this is just a phase
   and that you continue to grow.

I too, had misplaced hatred
   and couldn't see it in myself.
I thought for me to be more,
   others had to be less.

I didn't think my own wings
  would enable me to fly
  so I threw shade on others
  who prevailed in taking flight.

We all have times in our past
  for which we aren't very proud.
We all have current struggles
  right here in the here and now.

I embrace my present joy
  and resist future complacency.
A life absent growth and change
  seems absolute absurdity.

These words of truth and caution
  come from someone far from perfect,
  someone spiritually ambitious.
For that, I am unapologetic.

2 - What I Owe

I owe a lot of people
  because I didn't get here by myself.
Through the worst times of my life,
  I was still greatly blessed.

It only takes a fraction of thought
  for me to become overwhelmed-
  when I think about all the people
  who helped me be who I am.
They saw pass my pain
  and all the chaos that it wrought.
They helped me carry my burden.
They helped me assuage the cost.

When I was living off the grid,
  some blessed me with food to eat.
Some gave me rides when needed.
Some gave me a place to sleep.
A few even tucked me in at night
  so my body and soul could rest.
When my bodily functions went haywire,
  a few cleaned up my mess.

I'll never forget...
The frenemy who offered her lovely place
  so I could have privacy to withdraw.
The nursing student who coached me through it
  and every coworker who cheered me on.
A hard conversation with a dear friend
  held through his tearful eyes-
  who knew me before my addiction.

He tried desperately to set me right.
A good friend took me one night
  to sit by the pond at Byrd Park
  so I could soak in all the peacefulness
  and release some tears under the stars.

I can't count the people who were there for me.
They strengthened my will to fight.
In the darkness of self destruction,
  their deeds provided light.

They held back all their judgment
  but never spared their love.
I was constantly encouraged
  that who I was was already enough.
They shared some of their stories
  so I'd know I wasn't alone
  and used themselves as examples
  to help me regain my hope.

They assured me I was worthwhile
  when I didn't think I merited effort.
They went way out of their way
  to make at least one day better.
They instilled in me the confidence
  that in the world, good still exists.
That maybe it was time to fight
  and my addiction, I could resist.

They didn't have to lift a finger
  yet they offered me a hand.
They were in no way obligated
  to help me lift my head.
God often sends his other children

as angels to aid and save you.
Had it not been for their love,
  I never would have made it.

You may never know how your goodness
  will uplift a weakened soul.
You may never witness the fruit
  from the seed that you planted bore.
Some, I'll never see again.
Most, I ain't seen since then.
I owe it to their love and efforts
  to be the best person that I can.

We all are in debt to someone.
No one can do it all alone.
Whenever kindness finds you,
  repay it by passing it on.

3 - My Family's Fault

Families fuss and fight at times.
That fact is nothing new.
It happens in the one you're born in
  and in the ones you choose.

Most of us have been through times
  when home didn't seem like home.
All families tread through things
  capable of exacting terrible tolls.

In plucking out all my splinters
  so my traveling feet can last,
  I had to dig deep in myself
  and reckon with my past.

I had to deal with some issues
  in which others may have played a part.
It's not about casting blame
  but the full healing of my heart.

It's solely my side of my story.
Others have their own point of view.
Though perspectives are bound to vary,
  the love is not up for dispute.

Families are mostly people,
  so things are going to go wrong.
It's because we all come with faults,
  not due to a lack of love.

I say this for anyone whose family

is as imperfect as families can be.
And since God did all the creating,
  my imperfect family is perfect for me.

I wouldn't be who I am
  if they weren't who they are.
Everything my family has given me
  outweighs any hurt by far.

Sometimes folks hold on to hurt
  that was accidentally inflicted.
They think it will harm the family
  if the truth is fully admitted.

They can't pluck out their splinters
  because their pride causes denial.
They struggle to move forward
  burdened by the pains that bind them.

My family's bond is too strong for that.
It's withstood its share of tests.
Our loyalty can endure any process
  that leads to our best selves.

My family knows I love them.
Of them, I'm solidly proud.
I've worked on many of my issues
  and am focused on the here and now.

I'm sealing up the cracks
  and fortifying my base.
I'll need solid footing
  to continue running my race.

My family will be cheering me on
  and will catch me should I fall.
I know this with complete certainty
  because they've been here through it all.

4 - In Taurean's Light (Part 2): The Whole Time

Chicken fingers, fries with honey mustard.
For years, by that meal I was haunted.
Any time we'd order out,
　it was all Taurean wanted.

Baseball fields and school yards,
　the playing of a certain song.
There was nowhere I could escape
　the daily reminders brother was gone.

It didn't take much to set me off.
My soul had been ripped to shreds.
Surviving each day became a chore.
Forget about one more year.

Everything was much too much-
　even normal, everyday things.
Coping was nonexistent,
　then entered the dreams.

I recall only one as a nightmare
　and boy, that bitch was tough.
He was screaming and crying out to me.
He was pinned underneath his car.
As my brother pleaded to me
　to come and save his life,
　he changed from baby to boy to man-
　images from his short time.

That nightmare did a number on me.
Not only was my brother gone-

it made me think of the pain he was in
and that his last breath was taken alone.

The dreams were real and vivid,
　as if he'd never left.
There was one about his wedding day-
　a day he would never get.

There was one where I was being rough
　and accidentally made him cry.
I hated that I caused his tears.
I apologized and hugged him tight.
When I woke the next morning,
　I could still feel his warmth in my arms.
Then in horror it set in again-
　the sweet baby boy was gone.

Most of my dreams were beautiful.
I was close to him again.
The problem is very obvious.
In the mornings, my dreams would end.

Each time grew more devastating-
　that repeatedly, I had to discover
　that Taurean was truly dead.
There was no coming back for brother.

Every morning after dreaming of him,
　I would awake to the cold, hard truth.
In 2001, he died at 18
　and there was nothing big sister could do.

With every dream it got harder
　to again say a forever good bye.

I didn't want to face the next day
  just to relive finding out he died.

I couldn't handle no more next mornings
  but everyone has to sleep.
With great guilt I begged the Lord
  to please take these dreams from me.

It had to be a decade that passed
  that I didn't recall him as I slumbered.
Was he hurt by my rejection?
Full of shame, I often wondered.
.
Did he think I was angry with him
  that I had to push him away?
Did he know that I'd do anything
  for him to live just one more day?

Then one night as I slept,
  I dreamt that I was on the job.
I was rolling making money,
  straight getting my hustle on.

As I was handling my business,
  I felt like I was being watched.
I didn't have time to look around.
I didn't have a moment to stop.
I was ringing in an order
  in a computer by the stairs.
A figure slowly descended them.
It was Taurean standing there.

I shrieked with joy when I saw him.
It was magic to weary eyes.

He deserved my full attention
  so I begged for a little more time.

I hurried through with my duties,
  rushing before he went away.
My brother had come for a visit
  but I knew that he could not stay.

I told him I loved and missed him.
I had so much to ask and share.
I asked if he'd been watching me
  and how long had he been there.

Taurean inhaled deeply.
He stared for a second then smiled.
He replied, "Sister, don't you know?
I've been here this whole time."

With that, the dream was over.
I immediately woke from my sleep.
Not a single one of the words I know
  can describe the morning's joy and peace.

Taurean was in no way angry
  that I pushed him out of my dreams.
It was quite the opposite,
  my brother came to see about me.

He visits me more often these days.
It's not as hard to say goodbye.
My dreams are now peaceful reminders,
  that he's always been by my side.

5 - Eggshell Boo

I wouldn't scale a mountain
  composed of poisons and toxins.
I wouldn't construct my floors
  with rusty, nail ridden boards.
I wouldn't set sail in an ocean
  made of venomous potions.
I wouldn't journey on a road
  paved with bombs that explode.
I wouldn't fly in a plane
  certain to burst into flames.

Those senseless things...
  I just wouldn't do.
I'm not into hurting myself for anyone
  and that anyone includes you.
So...although I could manage,
  I won't accept your damage.
I can't be your Eggshell Boo.

Like little broken eggshells,
  some of your ways
  cause surprising harm.
I won't wait for things to worsen
  before I heed
  my gut's alarm.

These pretty feet weren't made
  to travel on eggshells
  or any other broken mess
  you throw down.
These pretty feet weren't made

for no eggshells
or anything else
that pollutes my ground.

Why would I choose
to become accustomed
to such pain, hurt, and suffering
when I've pledged to accept nothing
that will hinder my evolving?

I won't take kindly to condescension
or a constant line of questioning.
I won't stiffen up to be your trophy.
I'll cuss loudly and when I want to.

I won't play dainty when I eat.
I might even snort when I laugh.
I'll go when and where I please.
I won't be talked down from my path.

I'll exhibit my full range of emotions.
I must freely think just as I breathe.
As long as it's my decision,
I'll enjoy each and all of my me's.

And I can't do that living on eggshells...
tiptoeing my way through life,
trying to avoid your broken pieces
that cut as sharply as any knife.

I'd surely select a rose's petals
before I would choose its thorns-
something exquisitely soft and silky
to adorn my sanctuary floors.

Definitely nothing that will injure me
  or cause me to become untimely worn.
Though I can't control the world outside,
  I'm certainly queen in my home.

Don't matter your reasons...
  whether broken dreams or shattered schemes.
Or maybe you were just raised
  to see women in a certain space.
Maybe it's a need to be in charge
  and to always appear hard.
And since none of that is love,
  there is nothing more to discuss.

Therefore, I must kindly bid adieu.
I just can't. I ain't having it.
I just can't be your Eggshell Boo.

6 - My Dopeness

Don't try and pick it up
  if you can't hold it,
  if you have too many leaks
  and your vessel ain't solid.

It's my dopeness
  and it is for real.
It is heavy, strong, fierce and steady,
  a magical potion of mythical proportions.
Not everyone can handle a mixture so potent.
So don't try to pick it up
  if you can't hold it.

My dopeness is monumental.
I stand on the shoulders of survivors,
  innovators, game changers and warriors.
I know from where
  and from whom I come.
Even with my high powered imagination,
  I can not behold the spectacular potential
  of which God has made me capable.

My dopeness is 10 dimensional.
It comes at you from angles
  you didn't know existed until
  my essence flooded your territory
  and you had to take me in
  to try and comprehend my effect.
To not be perplexed
  by this powerful energy I reflect.

My dopeness is elemental.
It is as natural as natural can get.
It is the fundamental thing to great matters.
My dopeness spans the universe and
  can not be broken down.
Its makeup is not conducive to imitation.
A miraculous event
  that requires its own science.
A unique configuration and
  there is no denying it.

My dopeness is electric, kinetic,
  magnetic, in fact, quite prophetic
  and by all definitions,
  unapologetic.
It will exist and strive
  with or without your saying so.
It adds light and positive energy
  wherever it goes.
Its shine just might blind you.

My dopeness will persist
  and is not relegated to
  the limits of this list.
Though it was planted from my beginning,
  it didn't grow like this overnight.
Pain into power, I defined my fight
  and made it my business
  to not be led by sight.
By faith instead,
  I patterned my walk.
I centered my eyes
  on that vision from God.

My dopeness is not in competition with yours.
Each has its own plane of existence,
  cultivates its own space,
  makes and breaks its own rules.
There is more than enough room for all of us.

Your dopeness...
That, you must discover for yourself.
Don't be afraid to travel
  to the darkest places of your own being
    where many of your dope qualities and strengths
    remain dormant until you call them by name.
They are waiting on you to light a spark
  so they can catch full flame.

I will be as excited to embrace your dopeness
  as I have been to embrace my own.
God created all this dopeness
  and He didn't create it to exist alone.

7 - Dancing Shoes

This poem isn't about dancing shoes
  even though it kinda is.
It's more about losing parts of myself
  because that's exactly what I did.

It's funny that a trip to the closet
  took me to the way back when.
It led me back to a place
  that I had long since been.
The closet is where I spotted them,
  those old dancing shoes of mine.
I tried them on to test their fit
  and began a journey through time.

I would put on some dancing shoes
  every Friday and Saturday night.
Minutes after getting off work,
  to the dance floor, I'd take flight.
Complete with a stash of clothes,
  no time to go home and change.
All of me had to answer
  when the dance floor called my name.
Bright lights pulsating overhead
  as the music stirred my soul.
The whole vibe of the club
  was an escape to a fantasy world.

A place of joy and happiness.
A place to let my spirit flow.
A place to shake loose some problems
  until I couldn't shake no more.

A healthy way to decompress.
A sexy way to relieve some stress.
It didn't matter who was watching,
  I was just simply being myself.

I'd be surrounded by mostly twenty somethings.
Some asked if I'd teach them my moves.
I told them I was doing nothing special,
  just enjoying my own natural groove.
I wasn't dancing to be seen.
I was just doing what made me feel free.

I couldn't recall when I last wore those shoes
  or danced my blues away.
Long gone was my huge stereo
  and my favorite music to play.
I let that me slip away from myself
  when on a new mission I embarked.
Never did it even occur to me
  that from myself, I could get so far.

Music had always been important,
  an integral part of my life.
I missed that me so much
  that I danced my ass off that night.
I took my cell and some headphones
  and found some favorite tunes.
I made my whole place a dance floor
  and rediscovered my former groove.
I have since...
  reinstated Candice Caroake Dance Party.
It has returned to a regular thing.
I pledge to carve out time for it
  and to cherish how it makes me feel.

8 - Toenails

Help me paint my toenails
  or sit while I braid my hair.
Please just spend some time with me
  as I bless my temple with care.
Help me paint my toenails
  so I can tell You about my day.
Please curl up next to me
  to hear what I have to say.
Even when what I need to say
  is not what You want to hear.
Even when life's overwhelmed me
  and to myself, I'm not even clear.

You don't have to be here.
Not a thing to me, do You owe
  but Your presence calms and soothes me
  and there is nothing like it in this world.
Help me paint my toenails.
You don't have to touch the brush.
Just be here while I coat them,
  that would be more than enough.

Let me bounce the things off You
  that have filled up my vast mind,
  even when my emotions have run amok
  and the words I'm unable to find.

Let me not suppress my anger
  or deny my hate and fear.
Help me to not shut down inside,
  to numb how I feel.

Don't let me run away
　or hide from the brutal challenge.
Walk with me as I journey through life.
With You by my side, I can manage.

Help me paint my toenails
　and I will thank You for my feet.
Sit here with me long enough
　and I will thank You for everything.
Please sit as I paint my toenails
　or maybe while I curl my hair.
Any task becomes more beautiful
　knowing that You are there.

But I especially love Your company
　as I tend to my pretty feet.
I'm most reminded while I paint them
　of the work You put into me.
That this masterpiece wasn't random
　but a unique and beautiful design
　and that these chocolate feet have carried me
　many a wondrous mile.

I think about the sites
　that I've seen along the way.
I think about the obstacles
　that You have held at bay.
I think about the other travelers
　following their own paths.
And I am grateful for all I've done
　and grateful for all I have.

Sooo...
Help me paint my toenails

as I assign words to my thoughts.
Indulge me with Your company
  as my mind goes near and far.
Moments like these are my favorites.
They're made up of the little things.
While the world spins around Lord,
  please paint my toenails with me.

9 - When the Dust Settles

When the dust settles
 who will I be?
Will I be so changed
 I don't recognize me?

Will being a new person
 help me traverse my path?
Will I love this new me
 as much as the last?

When I survey my surroundings,
 will I finally feel free?
Will I have grown something beautiful
 from all of my seeds?

Will I have made precious peace
 with what can't be undone?
Will I at last be satisfied
 with all that I've won?

Change is required
 to breech the next level.
I summon the courage
 to make myself better.

I summon the bravery
 to admit I need work.
I pray for God's vision
 to live as I'm worth.

Spiritual ambition

has always been there.
I summon the strength
  to climb every stair.

I summon the resolve
  to burst through the doors.
I summon self love
  to declare inner war.

Endless uncertainties
  present resistance to change
  but the fighter in me
  persists by my faith.

The ambition of my spirit
  commands evolution.
Breaking old patterns
  compels revolution.

The biggest battles I've faced
  have been waged inside.
I've used the light of my gift
  as an unwavering guide.

I trust in God's love.
I'll believe the whole way.
Though I'm still trying to learn
  how to live day by day.

I will live by God's promise
  and make the most of my existence.
What I demand of myself
  will make all the difference.

When the dust settles,
  I will emerge and take flight.
The purpose of spiritual warfare-
  to ascend to new heights.

Alphabetical Index of Poems

Acceptable Dose, An	81
Automatic Entry	58
Black Versus Black	55
Climb, The	16
Company We Keep, The	29
Crack in My Foundation	13
Dancing Shoes	120
Devil's Most Wanted	10
Do Me No Favors	96
Eggshell Boo	114
Fat, Black, and Smart: The Acquisition of Adjectives	63
FIGHT!	93
In Taurean's Light (Part 2): The Whole Time	110
It Was The Laughter	52
Killah at the Door	6
Land Creature	24
Most Detrimental, The	75
My Chocolate Palm	3
My Dopeness	117
My Family's Fault	107
Not That Kind of Fence	78
One Enemy	90
Peace of My Pieces	45
Persistent Caller, The	84
Prime Directive, The	48
Required Role, A	38
Sorry Set Me Free	20
Stopped By The Light	41
Tainted	71
Tap In	87
Toenails	122
Toxic Ties (Never Too Late)	35

Unapologetic Ambition..101
What I Owe..104
When the Dust Settles...125
While I Cry..43
Will To Change..27